I STILL GO TO BED WITH WATER

By Melanie Sevcenko

Attention schools, libraries, and businesses: this title can be ordered
through Ingram. For special sales, email sales@unsolicitedpress.com.

For information contact:
Unsolicited Press
Portland, Oregon
www.unsolicitedpress.com
orders@unsolicitedpress.com
619-354-8005

Original Photo Credit: Sebastian Schobbert/Artur/VIEW
Book Design: Ryan Obermeyer
Editor: Alexandra Lindenmuth
ISBN: 978-1-956692-32-7

Table of Contents

Empty Cup

There is a cup crying out to be filled with the dried oils
that paint the room so starkly.

There is a sky praying to be knocked upon, voyaging so close
to bowing heads in the airport park, teasing arms with

the notion that to reach out and touch it is to Hail,
to die big and blessedly simple on the outside of the earth.

There comes death, disguised as light,
seeping through the slim horizon at the bottom of the door

thickening to massacre the dark stillness of the room
with full white motion.

She has known her dead, felt them since childhood,
resting her head against the glass pane in the backseat

reading her singing lips in the reflection,
rushing through a cottony storm of the shavings of stars

that cups the coal black highway as an overturned container
losing its liquid.

There is a frail thing in a movie theater, tapping you on the shoulder to tell you it's dying

when you turn around in the glow of the projector
to see it smiling and cupping handfuls of dried stems

just before it does.

I Can Hear the Sea

After a day on the ebb,
I can hear the sea trickling in.
It's up to no good, summoning strollers

to cross its bridge of boulders
as the long-absent sun finally turns
its hot slapped face to us.

I see salty tears filling
damp cheeks of sand
kissed by spring-heeled feet

a wet muttering mouth
closing in on the walkers
leaving them stranded against its

wild-flowered island. I'm nervous, as
I've been here before, three rocks south
of this calamity.

I know the heart that freezes when it's
truly alone, when not even the wind can
be found, after nature has gone stale.

There was nothing but Celtic configurations,
stone Jesuses, cursive paths crossing out
patches of parched yellows.

I was a wee mouse, faceless, heartless.
To exist was to scurry on instinct.
I was others, too.

I was my cousins. I built a pub in Gory, Ireland.
I swept dust into cracked floorboards.
I raised five daughters.

I drove my wife to the salon. I believed in God.
I hitched down to Waterford.
I stoked cattle and I ate them too.

I met my ghost in the fireplace. I turned
my head to the window. I knew the
leaves as brothers.

I chewed their plum to the pit and left it
on the nightstand under spilt light
of squash mellow

where it sat as its own
tiny world on wood

dry as the tide in retreat.

Mengele's Lake House

When we are shameless,
you part my legs in the dirty lake
once mixed with the blood of soldiers
        from some battle.

It's hard to tell them apart when most surfaces here
have held the back of a dying man of war.

Its mad doctor once owned this house by the lake:
his experiments locked into closets
long before some Secretary of the Allies
awarded medals on the lawn
long after the gurneys were wiped down
            the cords pulled from the electrical sockets.

I don't remember the name of the Secretary
but I do remember the lawn, its dry fibers
scratching my bare back
        my bikini top long gone.

I, a fallen soldier under you,
        rubbing the loose earth of summer into your face
            determined to make it home.

And you, my brother, enflamed by courage
                    hands oiled in my bleeding heart.

Somewhere, on the other side of this lawn,
beside the moon dimpled lake
       an old friend recites this history.
Beside him the stereo yawns over the sandwich-wrapped water:
       Then if it don't work out,
               then you can tell me goodbye.
       Then if it don't work out,
               then you can tell me goodbye.

Radiating the Strata

1.

'At midnight the veil is the thinnest,'
        you turned to me
in Halloween's torrential rain.

Us, feral creatures,
        scuttled around the water tower
at the end of your street

friends for half our lives, sisters
        caked in face paint,
your mouth stitched shut with eye liner.

Black silks and nylon wigs
        summoning Goddesses through your drunk fog
to put our lives right
        the way they were intended

                where our men are new and committed
                        as the Bodhisattva.

2.

The night we smoked opium in North Texas
        and dragged the dozy dealer to the porch:
we fell asleep to your new folk boyfriend.

With the cassette well run
        I heard his voice
                murmuring hub and bub

from the coffee nook
        in sync with your morning coos
                like small laughter,

not the smacking spittle
                of a dawning tongue.
Each morning the sun shot down
        armfuls of its stuff

and each night we played that game
                with our superpowers
which we tested in your car
in your parents' garage
when your roommate wasn't home

                radiating the strata —
our favorites: cyan, chartreuse, malachite,
        razzmatazz.

3.

We were famous:
we were the Dead Kids.

      Hecate, Sedna, Cerridwen and Persephone —
they've nursed us through the Maiden phase,

    and they'll be there
    when we're croning.

I felt them the night you were married,
    all of us reunited in your stepfather's limousine.

      The rainbow lights
super-powering
    through the tainted windshield.

The driver knew the way. I did not.
In the fuselage of booze sweat and gowns,
      I asked, 'Is this the afterlife?'

    'Yes,' you turned to me,
    your grinning mouth

stitched shut with eye liner.

Saint Kastanien Will Free You

How come I am always in a house?
We speak only to split time asunder
       even my friends know my dinners before they are cooked.
Just once around my nose it smelled of heroin.
Do the edge a favor and take the plunge.
Yesterday three dogs
were walked on my block
       three tastes go into one wrap.
Blush for the sun. He can't spend days in a treehouse
       built by the mock uncle you loathe.
A little one crawls from under his urges.
Cross 'em bridges and slap your scalp.
       Can we ever trip without an additive?
       Do childhood carpets always smell like doll piss?
       Will my end be the birth of a model push-up?
I jump at false starts and sour records.
I am done with the art of cruelly
hoarding my un-doneness.
I am spiraling
       myself out.

Six Months at Most

I divulged,
I'd only be gone a short time, six months at most.

But along the way my spirit got tripped up.
She is always talking & bringing digestibles

to her cracked lips, staining them red with wine
bruising her lungs on the inhale.

She is constantly packing her bag & unpacking
accumulating plants, herbs, papers

& other things that
take root, like her vanity.

I've tugged her, nudged her, spelled it out:
         we must go to complete the memory.

But each time I let in the coordinated spirits –
spooling bobbin, threading our private maps

underneath – her thoughts cater selfishly
to the scenes she will bridge

a triangulation of muses
every way she loves

that which winks at her in gratitude
from its own wounded spot on the floor.

In summer, I agree to join her at the city's shores,
but come winter I don the heavy boots

hold up in the house
plot next year's garden on graph paper

mount tea & paper
on the white walls of my singularity

season the soup with the coarse pepper
of my remains, wrap her in another bundle of wool

burn the strips of white paper wishes by candle
say goodnight to family.

Everyone should have a house by the river. Everyone
should grow so old & sleep into death.

Where Nostalgia

cannot hurt them is how

they pass the hours

holding their breath

into the black distortion

shooting down arid highways

under the starless sky

that glows with the stamina of parking lots

whose concrete never lets the soles of sneakers foul

whose nights smell of chlorine and heat

and carry the names of showered

tanned young women

called Trish and Marcy

whose made-up faces never smudge

in the lamps

of pedestrian plazas.

On a Platform

1.

Passing through this
old one   old suit   dawdler
     lover   our coats did meet on a platform.
Some say the way we laughed was a parking lot of shifty
shopping carts   our girl said a God fire
     but I'm only familiar with this choir tone.

Remember that night we exchanged books
and I perused your poetry between course kits
to learn your lecture style.

In the off-time, you'd make smoke rings and shoot dormitory things
through them:
     wool hat   laundry soap   plaid fabric
        my dial tone   snowflakes on the bottle rims
     below us.
Passing notes that no doubt felt better as whispers.

But I never had a wispy throat to woe you.
     On those platforms, mashing winter layers together
I would have gladly sought the blood of lambs

who gave your jacket its lining
      just to get closer to your
            navy top and army bottom.

2.

Your two mates, don't forget
asking for grass behind my shoulder blades
while we watched the National Film Board dedicate a poet
      who washed himself in Buddhist blankness.

Later, in the screening room, we found your boys
      barricaded in cardboard
cocking weaponry of towel and toilet tubes. It didn't matter
that God now glanced back to see what he'd tripped on:
      a bowlful.

3.

When tidings came, we took to Christmas carol transparencies
      conducted by principals from gymnasium walls.
We tore up every scrap of signage   jumped in their piles
raked them back up   desecrated the graduates
      pulled colored threads from college scarves
                  cursed specialization
concluded the consciousness of the spider

made breakfast in aluminum   drew campfires from corners
to raise the souls of kosher deli hangover sluts

swallowed the decibels until we figured
     -8 was our peak.

Slam-danced in nod-offs   threw desks at blackboards
peep-showed the potheads   left messages for the hierarchy
     left offerings for the janitor in a wreath of butts and ash.

We went Cuban all the way with no visual aid
and found the ship encasing in the classroom
but always from inside the institute
     all to avoid the outside.

Southern Gothic

What needed to
          came undone that night
on the porches of Southern Gothic.
An albino raccoon made an appearance

its eyes bright
          flat like nickels lit in the rain.
It slinked under the railing and ducked
into a shrub. You slid a bracelet off your

wrist and onto mine. It was made of tabs
from soda cans, strung together with white elastic.
It's the only thing you've ever given me.

Things got said, things got drunk.

We caught each other's slumped heads
and I waited for your hands to keep talking.

Instead, we listened to ghost stories from the shit
that crawled out of our depraved hearts.

'It's like some old hurt that sneaks up from behind
       and chokes you out,'
              was something that came from you

I'd like to think I gave you the raccoon.

Morning Dew

Just when there seemed no way around
        young friends growing cancers
                resting lovers returning to the flight

or that precious
        babbling slit

that crashes into my mouth
        and chains me to its oniony lies,

then it comes like morning dew:

a shimmer
        more dapper than a hooked arm in escort

allowing us
        to radically accept
                everything that led us to this:

the blinking yellow arrows / the language of grandparents we
never learned / our cystic ovaries / the pins and needles
in our fetal positions / our hairy female chins / our bipolar
boyfriends / age that binges on our birthdays.

But it lasts only as long as
                moisture on a leaf
      before returning to the insect's throat.

Back inside where it's blind and idle
      we are penniless, title-less.

until dawn peaks —
      a nascent dew coos the storm-tossed night

our pretty humming skulls
      captured in its beads.

The Systems

1.

That a dream can disturb an entire day
rotten wreck on the brain
turning relations against each other
or drawing those in
who were never supposed to be near.

Each cell of my spider consciousness spins a web
and each night I catch him.

In the right-sided light, his head is a singer's
a fog of song drops from this mouth
        and in the left, his body pink as a virgin prince.
From behind he is taller
than all the Turkish men on the sidewalk
outside their businesses
smoking in front of commuters
knowing nothing of my past with him
how we disappeared in the thicket of the opposite coast
with the tumor hiding in his chest
a deserted golf ball, riding out winter in the hole
an insect, gone mummy on the web.

2.

No one had ever questioned my electromagnetic field
all those nights when I broke all the glasses
all the drying dishes, drenched the walls in wine.
I knew it must be off, scattered —
a child scrambling stations, frying stereos, jamming software.
Sometimes I'd fall out of my body, perplexed by who
I was forced to carry from one day to another.

The city that crumbled in the war now burns with spirited fire.
It keeps glasses filled because no one wants to be alone anymore.
When we pass the glasses between each other
they break, and I go to my knees.
The liquid in my body leaks.
It wants to join the mess on the floor.

3.

On the Redwood deck
I'm left rearranging this life
without interpretive technology.
All this biology cannot exist a plane's distance above us.
We know how fussy our systems have become
because we've reached beyond them
in special suits with breathing apparatuses.

On the forest floor it gets confusing
to not have the nomenclature

to name each piece at my feet.
So I don my robotized legs which categorize
everything they step on
slippery detritus between metal toes.
Underneath I am mostly water sealed in flaky skin
a thing that crunches when it receives big hugs.
But I move it forward.
I thought I've been walking it off my entire life
(maybe the length of a country by now)
maybe not enough.

4.

The city built a new system, it dings with factory productivity
it smells like where industry meets backyards
it's innocent and aesthetic like public transportation.

The commuters come, they tote briefcases with shoulder straps.
(Most own technology I never will have.)
Their cheeks are alive with curiosity, they work themselves into it
with permanence, as though nothing were temporary.
It takes them home.
It will be there (on time) when they rise each morning.

From each house there are little things:
a cough, an instrument, paper lanterns that ignite the porch
in billboard pose. I glide past them
my hair finally cut short (I've wanted this since high school)
a mute radio in my basket.

Whoever has these houses now
will always have these houses.
Whoever is out of fashion
will stay out of fashion.

Practical Beach

I found you asleep beside the tide.

I woke you with a bundle of fruit.

We shared a plum and wiped the juice from our chins.

I sucked a date down to its pit, then asked if you liked dates.

You looked confused, assuming I meant

a meeting of two potential lovers.

I produced the seed, you questioned

whether I had pulled it from the stone fruit.

No, this kind of date, I said

showing you the brown bag where their sticky

brothers lumped together like cockroaches.

You asked me what color I thought the sea was.

Navy blue to match the sky.

We moved 'round the spheres of our jobs and education

and admired the coating of lives lived in all ways

as your feet sank deeper into sand.

> Then I thought, somewhere, something is stirring
> the still beneath us
> into a murmur

Baltic spirits gave your second language a slur.

Even so, your intoxicated English was truer

than the map to this practical beach

where you made up for the ocean's

unwillingness to woo me.

Flat White

On these sheets   my bodily functions
are meticulously recorded
sending me shuffling down the hall
to the eek of the bathroom light
cutting my gait to a limp

because the fault I feed my flesh
is one of soft   safe pain
because on the opposite side of the earth
they are canceling out the sick part of your brain
with a radio beam.

We must meet on a literal hot island
between us   when this is over
when each day on your calendar bears a weight
while retaining freedom.

We will beach and watch young women in grass skirts
drink flat whites   and speak German again
to the oil-slicked businessman   and not talk about

time. Such conversation is for home.
I know a young woman who closes her door and tears
her room apart   betrayed by the dreams
she whispered into a cup   a mold she cast
when she flipped over the card   the pattern it held.

Beyond her door is me   never drawing comfort
from the sugar   never negating the
instant end   on the edge of everything

following the stories of strangers like trails to
their doors. Inside   perversion rests in old trunks
family portraits as patches to peepholes.

I share a bed with the raw thing   it loves to
wake me in the night   my pupils panicking
making shapes and scenarios from the shadows
posing questions of death   I can't answer yet.

Beneath her door   I see paradise like this:
        your gray hair black again   moonlit water
        up to our necks   the radio beam restoring
        power to your brain.

Senefelder No. 2

The building that contains me now
is the stuff of post-war sci-fi
a relic of the Eastern Bloc
      that can't fit through the memory hole.

I hold a paperback   in my journeyed hands
that tells the same story   in the quiet of the studio.
This edition was given to me on my birthday
from a vendor in Mauer Park.

Resting my reading on the windowsill
I let my eyes fall
into the courtyard below
still attached to my mind
in a frail pulley system.

I once took a picture
from down there in the rain
framing up towards the highest windows
my lens blotting the building's
bleeding skins   peeling back
to reveal a Plattenbau rubbed raw.

I have one exposure left.
I will give it to the alley of willow trees
in the green park around the corner.

I spent three weeks in this flat
smoking beside the record player
letting Miles Davis in headphones
lead me to a dark snowfall.

Soundlessly it drifted down
when there was no horn
for a measure or more.
I walked back and forth
across the wood floorboards
swept them from time to time
and crouched at the tiny piles
of crunched up paper
to save the loose change.

So Quietly

So quietly I stalk the east side,
thinking how I may never
disembark these foot bridges,
the loom of his dreams
spinning out my own.

I walk and look at all ten of
my fingers like a family
of different heights & different lines.
A family I have not agreed to,
but they are my rogue bunch
nonetheless.

When I read of antiquated
middle-aged women
running scared into the night,
pushing through the desert air
to escape the lives they agreed to,

    I fear I see myself
    the whites of my eyes
    as bold as doves
    that spring from my sockets

and sail into the free open sky
as I clutch to their meaty feathers.

I have been warned:

love is the wind
stirring the grass
beneath trees on a
dark night.

Strangers Bewitched in the Power of Nothing

we had ordered milkshakes / the day we became powerless / a

parlor in Little Italy / the blenders had stopped / globs of cream

& sugar would not be spun into rich froth / that could coat our

stomachs / mine own had been churning / a chain of our

unspoken narratives / the shy longing we felt / in dry reeds / me

at the audio mixer / the awkward brushy kisses / at the end of

Brit Pop night / trying to wake you / for a ride to school / you /

twitching up through your narcolepsy / then we were powerless

/ watching street lamps burn out / popping Christmas lights on

a shitty fuse / cars veered to curbs / radio dials scanned for

answers / this could be the end of us / the neighborhood met in

needle park / waiting for sundown / when it finally fell / joint

smoke filled the denim blue sky / the aliens could take us / the

bomb could scorch us / savior signboards were drafted with

Sharpies / the ash of community would soon / blanket the

metroplex / mingling with trash fires / in our tiny city backyard

we took manual photos / in the dark / negotiated the F-stops /

then ventured forth / out the gate / every passing body / a

flickering shadow / and as shadows they were kinder / in candle light / bars gave away bottled beer / warm and depreciated / we embarked abandoned streetcars / becoming spooks / while the hooks swayed / against the drained cables above / whispering bodies formed rings 'round / street corners & lampposts / a renaissance fair / with no lute horse or hen / just urban bodies / warm on reserve / strangers bewitched in the power of nothing / a new type of modern silence / hum-less / wave-less / not made for steel convention / but mountain strong / when the lights came back on / disappointment snapped / static down the corridors / flint before the fire / the droning befell the city / the same source / we once believed / charged our capabilities / metered & mechanized / our lifelines / we went back to / electric stoves / stereos / TVs / & you went back to her / but in Little Italy / behind a glass storefront / in the afterglow / the blenders started back up / our melted ice cream / something stronger / sweeter / in the surge / bewitched for no one

Moving Day

You parked yourself in a seat
in a chair you threw in the perfect place
  in a room with cheap rent.
I knew at once you were suited for my pen.
You could not escape this
and I put something down
about your shoes in the forefront
and the way you took charge
  of the power-nap moment.

  The weather here takes me to that day
  blue walls laid down fresh
  an abundance of cardboard
  a truck you almost backed into brick.

Afterwards I made a promise
to sit in the blood of concentration each day.
At 4 p.m. I hope to find the sun
on my porch and think how you might
be at ease someplace too.

This is a rattle

      this is your hair under a hat for days

      no sight of water anywhere.

Though in time we feel that twist of skin

between a crook

which proclaims, with candor:

      We all move our bodies to try another chair

      a small sip of cheer

         a new way to cross our legs.

A Hollowed Bone

With a dark ear
come to hear new flutes

from a hollowed bone
come to taste novel hunger.

A cavernous gully
so damp, so deadened –

an interior against which
organisms have not rubbed their cells.

But we like the new places
no matter how barren.

They have no furniture
no holes to patch

from pictures hung.
No stench of love lost

or skin burned –
just small, palm small.

Neither cataloguing label
nor controversial sex.

Staking no territory, attached
to no limb, contained

and sequestering
curled in upon itself

as the seashell.
Mum within for no one

except maybe the ocean
for music's sake.

Connector I

From the glass connector above the campus
I wait for the tree branches to shoot snowflakes at me
from their frozen barrels.

In winter they are birch white,
fine cigarettes for smoking the forest
of my tobacconist.

All the while safe in my clear pod, counting the
crystals that hit the panes and dissolve
like the fashions beyond it.

I ease into the corduroy bench and advance
my capsule. The snowflakes play along as I
time warp to the next galaxy.

I am so still, knowing of only one thing:
that under this actual air is a tunnel through which
I have run with cables and lights, beside my only darling.

Above it, suspended in a glass longhouse,
I am between two buildings

one for environmentalists
        the other for biologists

where professions are pontificating and some mind
in either one might change the way we wear shoes
or our perception of God – the man at work.

He is really just your friend who drinks beer
with you on weeknights
nervously eyeing your t-shirt.

I'll keep plugging away until I find the right
combination by which to graduate
from the host or the sidekick with the hair.

Then I needn't be a ballerina or construct a cello
to win them over.

They will come to me at night in dreams of starlight

and I will convey them always in factories

sleeping in shadows.

And it'll be a farmer's privilege (or a soap maker's)

to smoke tea with me in a canoe

on a river in Quebec.

For now, am I wrong to assume

my blood has been replaced by wine

that my capsule is a popemobile, which

makes me singular while present

and protected from the street below

from people in fraudulent popemobiles, from

my heart to theirs?

Before I Swallowed It

Before I swallowed it   I would awake

each morning   knowing only my name

pondering how strange it was to be a powerless woman of

           (breathe) years old

           living in *(breathe)*

           as a part-time *(breathe)*.

I was my forefather   looking at a young woman who

rained all day   from bed to bus   intoxicated

against some railing   always cursing the moon.

When he shut his eyes   I slit them open.   When he

scrambled for darkness   I dragged him out

into the sun's wandering anniversary arms.

Before I swallowed it   I was screaming at the black outline

at the foot of the bed   my heart pumping hard

as the collective feet of a marathon race

a fuzzy swarm of pulsing dots on a data map   my cries

coming from only my name   an energy clinging

to the wrong body   with no memory of the room.

Before   I was a casing of hair and nails

        a mad pestilence that displaced the person

eating as an animal   on the kitchen floor at night

        never swallowing.

Swim-up Bar

Your ground floor balcony
like a swim-up bar
because your face is always
        golden tanned
                punch drunk.

I found your panic attack sunset
on Letná's river, washing over
        my pull-screen cityscape
– Gothic spires, Baroque core –
against the hum and click
        of the slide
                in the carousel.

I tell you about it on the floor
        in your blankets before the telly
watching Romancing the Stone.

When we were children
basic cable ran it
        back-to-back.

Maybe it's why I still
find my way towards emerald
        my mud-caked skin
            an earthbound allure
                    my flushed lips
            you mistake for tinted glass
                my words a condensation
with which
        you converse through fingertip writ.

I miss the sun already
        headed for sentencing
            – winter's flatline –
when you really feel the airplane
        in a crash-landing

like a sled upon
the sparse snow.

Westland Row

I am the building's only
sleeping tenant.

In my upstairs apartment
I shove dirty rags in the hovel
above the front entrance
to get them out of my life.

I shower where the hall closet
should have been, at the foot of
carpeted steps of royal blue.

I arrange the books here monochromatically
then marvel at our common heritage.

The plates and knives were all here
when I moved in. I make a clothesline

from a telephone cord and hang wet

towels on the fire escape for drying.

When the sun burns fierce

the railing's black paint attaches

to the fabric like dehydrated squid ink.

Across the roof the editors of a

socialist newspaper invite me

for cake and wine in celebration

of their 50th edition.

On the city's bridges I've met men

who call the River Liffey sexy

in Saturday's nightfulness.

Come Sunday I skip over

puddles of party bile.

I know no one 'cept for the cobble

of each stone to my temporary home.

In each frame could be my kin.

This is where a quarter of me began.

This is where my anger holds

a fifth of whiskey.

My Scottish neighbor who deals business

has placed potted plants

in his window

as to not see me

in the up and down of clothing

at the rise and falling of the sun.

Innocent Railway Tunnel

Entire seasons would turn into each other like pages
falling upon the sky's silk and changing it with an exhalation
while I let it sit there – half underground, soiled and damp –
an empty grave with only vacationing souls. Constantly
it would summon cyclists, or schoolboys in neckties who
sought its melancholy and convenient passage. Until one day
I entered it, a coolness enfolded me, my life became open
at each end. And on the darkling path, between two
apertures eclipsed, it was there I was being born. Finally
crowning its light, my lungs were kissed with meadow air.
Crying out to get closer to the source, they leapt from my
breast and took their place amongst soft petals. I remained
well bled from the missing part, on my knees, but
surrounded by such sweet fragrance.

Litany for Spring

It was everywhere back then
and because we walked through it
    like odorless gas
    it found its way inside us
        changing our cells without permission.

It drew my face shut
    chewed the milk from my glands
left shadows of tumors
    and brought the maniac inside.

It filled the chasm above carpeted steps
    between bedroom and sitting room

        where the tones of parents' violent silence
        hangs and rises like hot air.

It owned every entrance of spring
    when the earth sells all of winter's souvenirs.

There were no words to speak then

    so the TV and radios babbled as we couldn't.

And the guest chairs filled with specialists

    who put pain in context.

Until I sundered the companion

    straightened my hunch.

My water-logged stacks of sorrow

       that once held me like a groom

          all sorted and slotted.

My hands have dropped their fat

    my fingers have let fall their fists.

       My smile is jowly.

This belly is full of a batch of newly

    swallowed flavors.

Death is also life, serpentine,

    like the voice and its instrument.

I find it in faces now, on pages I never wrote

on the shoulder of roads

in the weight of a rock so heavy it's stuck

with only one view of the world.

My own is wiped clean.

I once caught a seagull in the night sky

to show a friend how much

it resembled a skipping stone

whose trajectory is more magic

than teeth and lips.

I Still Go to Bed with Water

I am eight years old. I am lying
in my bed at night.

When I close my eyes, the sheets lose their
cotton quality, dampening in a coolness.

The bed wobbles like sea water beneath my steady
breath. I am floating, rafting over waves.

The seagulls my uncle threw dinner rolls to
squawk in the vague space above me.

Now fully grown, I still go to bed with water
after daylight hours at its unfurled ends

tangling me deeper into the cognitive sway.
When night falls here wood fires burn

in cylinders behind slack shanties
that reek of oil and drumming.

I like rooster calls in the soft distance
between the hot leaves of my well-noted life.

From Jerome

We might still be alive on the road through sullied homesteads
  besieged by cacti and their rusted garden parts –

but I'm not sure now, we're too far gone.
  The Albanians would call it, *where the wolves fuck.*

Chem-trails streak white across a matte blue sky
  with foamy, aerosol power.

This red rock we ride feels deposited from the future.
  Its silvers shower us in gifts

and we strip-mine its pits for history. At 4,000 feet
  my hands mimic rock guitar from the radio.

At turns, tiny crosses prick the body-shaped curves of the road
  that took all these lives.

Tarnished from backside sun, the crosses face
  snowy shoulders of highway

a religious divide between two temperatures. In town
  the locals compete to reach a higher consciousness.

They claim to be Masters or Shamans
      on the notice board of a corporate health food store.

At 5,000 feet, we wiggle and shift our bottoms in the car seat
      to ease our stinging lungs.

Beyond us, storefronts dangle from the edge.
      They sell painted wood, salt and crystals

to anyone
      who has not fallen off the town.

From blood to wine under Nevada moon
      peaking above the crooked jawline of mountain

the city's lights glisten like glass in the sand at its feet.
      All those people

each one a bright body on a dim sidewalk
      – dealing, nude and negated

when sky becomes ocean and earth crumbles clean
      to a chalky heaven.

Our car swallows the petrified highway, like a black silk scarf
      it gags on. A magic trick.

And the moon's in on it too, my hooligan on the right
      holding the headlamp of train robbery.

He has flooded Hoover Dam before
      he knows the way out.

And I confide in him: how abandoned we would feel
      without the spying of distant rocks.

The Way to Wood

You wail outside the gospel ring
'cos your calling heart
won't beat out a response

and croon to the vinyl children
of revolution
            from the fluorescents of the franchise.

When we chanted as mountaineers
under the mammoth black ice
we did it from our backyard tent.

We are all slowly becoming stars
            we're not instantly that way.

Inert as the labradorite
fallen from the frozen fire
of aurora borealis

            with all the convolution
            of iridescence
            just below the surface

I promise
it's just the weight of everything
that has kept you sidelined

ebbed as the river water
until you
gain momentum
          then drop
                    as the waterfall

casting sissy rainbow arches
above your boisterous

transporting mist.

In Poses

On the bus ride to the café
in my new town
I watch the water of a state river
lick its lips.
Its tea is poured.
And noting the vegetation
that tangled through all stone homes
along its bank
I knew I could wait for your beauty
if I had this to glimpse
in the meantime.

We rejoice in our craft
scaling the cave walls
behind every soft knowing
'til we find a common dialect
and hum it to each other
cheek-to-cheek.
Our history is what we make it.
I love to watch old men
hold one another
and I know you twinkle
at this too.

On the French side
a museum tells its visitors
to think of it as a canoe
from the inside.
I sailed within you
day and night
my museum you were.
Built with sand and stick
heaping with a narrowness
that taught me one lesson
one tiny display light at a time.

I wish I had an intensity to my face.
Is that what kept you distant from me?
I know a dancer whose eyes
I desire for my cradle
like two sacred gems
I rub in my pocket for magic.

I dreamed once that eyes gave
entirely too much away
leaving everyone's mouths open
in a perfect circle of horror
like a frozen angel choir.

I wish more often
we'd find ourselves
in poses

with smiles that
brightened in song
eyes that got wider
in competition of madness
limbs that flicked and ticked
and coaxed each other

nearer.

Business of Sadness

In the business of sadness
we walk to work.
You push your bicycle.
mine stays broken,
haunted in the courtyard.
Later, under a certain tree, you'll find me
'The Thrill Is Gone' between my teeth
my bottom lip sagging
but caught by the grace
of the sparrow's wing.
Your stony arms,
I have no ammunition against,
linger as empty buildings
from the fulcrum of your shoulders.
Your fingers as roof antennae
tuning me into the world.
They report the top stories
of necessary politics,
the squat life of an ivy league,
of Hungarian patriarchy.
These hands I fear
I will never let go of –
they know the art of patience

because you once touched a person
with the tip of one finger,
and it was more tender
than love making, you said.
So chin up, vodka down,
never fuck, ever.
Play on the songs of another
who stabbed his heart dead.
But we'll make it
because we know deconstruction
is no means to an end;
debating consciousness is a waste.
Death is merely waking up to a
silent house under snow.
Is it called flying when a crocodile
falls from a cliff?

Undertow

Few things have been as beautiful as the undertow
at the end of one Quebec waterfall

nipping the ankles of adolescents
narrowly close to drowning

then spitting us back through the lens
before the sunshine smiles of our picnicking mothers.

In the flushing gag of a memory,
I meet the ghosts that stalked his home and took him.

Our waterfall is dried up now,
its clay blown into future winds where he hangs

dusted gray
but in gestation – the imminent one.

When he returns, I will ask him to leave our youth alone
because nothing is simple in childhood

and nothing is more complex than a sad child,
and weren't we both solitary children?

In the interim, I must find him amongst the many
beyond a lonesome urban window

in the water that falls from the sky
like all of us do from some dark cloud

as prophets of lightning.

Short on Breath

1.

The weather had been
bothersome
this week, the days
trying their best
to crack open.
I think they knew
you were coming.
My throat had not been
swallowing like usual.
I think it knew
you were coming.
Your lung
forsook you, honey,
left you with only a lobe.
Short on breath,
we enter the house
where I am
the guest.

2.

Under a quilt,
my fingers
land on your cut
where they took out
part of your pump.
My heart, some
spirited beanstalk.
Nay! the rainforest's girth —
where you cheated
death six times
never knowing
you were dying
incrementally.
You had whores
on the world's
largest river,
you tell me.
Docked was your
boat, horny was
your crew.
You had them
in Reno too
after the surgery
when you started
breathing
on your own.

But you never
touched them,
you tell me,
because your arrogance
deemed them broken
like you,
and both parties
needed to
be heard.

3.

You tell me
the treatment center
was full of sagging
sick ghouls
in their 30s,
and you draw
your mouth
down and tight
like a slit.
I feel your back,
your stitched
scabby tracks
that led me here.
I unthread a piece of
your fine silk

just beneath
the skin
because you
ask me.
I pull it out
of you, watching
the translucent
new cells
rise over it
like a digesting
snake.

4.

Moments later
my menstruation begins,
staining a coin
on my pants
as we embrace
in this borrowed bed.
I, some salvation,
a pillared porch of your
Southern Gothic,
straddling a hilltop,
swinging a warm
gas light
in the storm.

Nay! a lighthouse –
anchored by many
sharp rocks
that may save
a drowning guest
who will enter,
changing me
like a new
sadness.

The Sun Opens its Eyelid

on afternoon's pillows
and somehow trouble seems bald.

Such exposure is open to interpretation
        because just when you lean back
        the bike breaks its crank
        the genes pop from the double helix
            like a wooden staircase beset by a gaggle
            of rough-housing kids
        as I come undone on a porch.

How many stutters in the sequence before a God
        seems dyscalculic?

Just drive five hours south to smell the forest fire
        see the hunger of the kill beetle
        how the choking vines
        grind to grist
            and feed all complex thoughts.

Once, I made a paper boat and filled it
        with the only grass from the suburb
            to commemorate my dead heroes.

Now, I need serotonin instead of seed.
I need a back float, a scorched summer foot, a box of wine
      a cool shade to rake my range
          back to order.

At a family lake, with more water than last season,
more glow than the lost camper's torch light:
      I spy two boys becoming two different men –
          one with a boy of his own.

Two men, loosening the choke of the vine,
      out to solve the equation of the new forest,
          under the wink of the sun.

Sleep City

Return to the city to sleep
end everything
by brushing my teeth.

You were right, abuser.
Closing my eyes
upon two steeples

two twigs of winter's famine
still rooted
above a manicured park

is the view
I'd like to go out on.
I push heart shapes

atop their spires, then
draw a crisscross of lines
against those squeaky

cherub curves.
Holy God, I have lost
my companion! I have lost

all my companions.
I kiss you invisibly &
express 'love yous'

before an extinguished
filter tip.
Useless —

more provincial politics
toppled upon me
by those legitimately

uninformed
— and I run to the hammer
as a nightfall solipsist.

Connector II

1.

Between academia and recklessness, we sit
          contained in glass, a storm not far off.

The wind is already throwing tree bark to the sidewalk
like unsatisfactory manuscripts
          with the weighty disapproval of anvils

while we remain protected by the suspended tube
nowhere really, just carpet below our
          bottoms and crossed legs.

Everything that is spoken now finds its way to heavy paper
every gesture now falls in step to the metronome
          of my dormitory. In there,
selected souvenirs of nuclear life, cradled
          but crestfallen
                    knitting headlines of adulthood and adultery.

2.

Is she lonely? Lonely as the hollow wood
marginalized to the creek
    splicing suburban foam
        forlorn in southern loam.

Lonely as the shotgun house
in the gutter of the rural highway
disappeared by tall dry grass
    the bodies decomposing in the
        audience of atoms.

Lonely as the chain link beside the fire
the homeless asking for a smile as currency
    when you haven't got a buck to your name.

3.

In the connector she sees weather from both sides
how it passes under and over her like road and sky
    pulling her roughly between party lines.

Everything beyond this glass is the first time she sees it.
    Her choices still feeling like choice

her ambitions plotted fresh upon the scorecard
       letters written by hand
              the Classics as steroids for her phrasing.

Fat fleshy face, oil paints staining virgin parts
       snow between her legs, barely a scar.

Death not always a hot stone in her palm
searing the tender lines
       to keep her grounded and wary.

Rage not yet a weapon turned inward
to laser cut her luck
       metabolize the fortune.

Under the Curtains

Remember your sister's refrigerator. Remember it had a
photo of your niece stuck to it. We drank your sister's
expensive carrot juice and you said, *You look like my
niece.* But she was 6 and we were 25. She had blond
curly locks and mine were brown. None of this had to
do with the fact that you looked like a combination of
all of my uncles, especially the one who knew about
constellations and collective dreaming because he
listened to talk radio at midnight when everything was
allowed to be mysterious. And how is it that years later
we ended up here? My pants down, the crown of my
head against the baseboard and under the curtains,
yours hidden in my jolly thighs. We were never to do
this again, we promised once: we are not 25 anymore,
we are not in America. We don't rip the belly out of
the night like we used to and toss it to the subway
tracks. We speak two languages now. We don't own
anything yet, but we'd like to. Remember back then

when the blue trees in Texas looked like a painting
against the night sky. Remember when their bark held
my back while you tore at my front. Sometimes I think
we're simply re-enacting that night in new scenarios.
Then I give and you take, like the night sky lets the day
disappear all the stars. I think all of this has to do with
the mysteries of midnight, because we can't fall to our
knees in subways, drunk on European blood. Instead
we settle for rug burn, where the baseboards are
always clean.

Landwehr

Come inside,
it's survived January's teeth
torn open to its bare anatomy
a branch system of sick ribs.
It's bedded half-smoked spliffs
sheltered three-legged dogs
and recited the soft platonic whispers of
re-rendered break-ups.

It's housed the dimes of tears
of those who elbowed at its swim-up bar.
It's judged devastated fashions and the riskiest footwear:
      Hausschuhe, winterized pumps,
          ankle twisters.

It's caressed the current and clenched its muscles
gone trapeze for the intoxicated passerby
who dared to swing and felt the lick of its canal.
It's sewn now with wisteria's twine and the
      ripe meat of young April buds.

Turn out the viscera,

       cough the quiet from your February chest

       clang your various selves together

       release your aimless melody.

       Reflect the light inward

       stretch the flesh outwards.

       Billow as the circus tent

       then welcome the town

       feed the elephants

       grease the ropes.

Listen for,

       the roll of winter's bone

       the arrows of thistle

       the shedded fur

       the bark's bark.

TX Exit

This is a brand new way to exit the state of Texas
turning over and stacking the town squares
to meet their compensations:
church baptizing in corporate pond
bank tower piercing strip mall
straight through the Dairy Queen.

The way out goes ten years back
with a long smoke
that took my eyes elsewhere
to the scurvy roads of thirsty brush
to the stereo that blesses bogus nature
to the bended meditation on family dinners.

Big bold bearer
          of hot white fire
we are still trying to escape it
literally east of Eden.
Leaving means taking from the few
we left behind, who will not ride out

the long straws of highways.
They stay where road signs
are the classifieds of bibles

    where the meth-bird sings

    cheering on queers who out-do each other

    in testimonials of hard liquor pickle backs.

Texas for ten hours
twinkles as an iridescent thread
in tightly woven bankrolls, leaving Mexico
on the other side with a heart attack.
Texas of Mother Mary
pasted to the center of the steering wheel
her blue folded scarf
teasing drylands
with the look of rain water.
She chases bumper stickers
branded with her immaculate Kid
and all the fish he caught
while hailin' rides with cowboys.
Out west we recycle dawns
growing colder still
from hot as hell.

Our Letters

Over time our letters have become
clearer reflections of stable life

less riffing from mountain clouds
less nights spent communing with
the rain's temper against a trailer window

breaking ice in whiskey
breaking our throats in sad sing-a-long
crafting from linoleum floors, wishing upon

that name rising each morning in the
positive space between the gathered trees.

You mark time now with the length of your hair
when trying to recall a love poem I once shared with you.

Am I allowed to doubt you, dear friend, as I
doubt the entry of spring on a March day?

We used to say the world was not put right:
our infinite lovers   belonged to others.

Before the Mirror

I catch my face on the brink of a fall.
A struck chord   in a casing
blown out the barrel. Last night's eyes
wet from a morning spill
now leave their skid marks swerved
'round a glassy wreck.

They have not read today.
The matching conversation is filed
between a thousand bindings.
What we do now is degrade our privileges
and summon everything to our mouths

gut our language and leave time to itself
deflated   collapsing upon its folds
because we neglect to exercise within it.
The goods we provide are simply piled
in a corner. A gateway has shriveled.
We putz.

We trade nothing for the satisfaction
of that which teases our lips.
No order is harnessed.
If I could encapsulate the grander goods
        those which come to me at the wheel
I would know what is worth spouting.

But it leaves me as soon as I release the handle
and my feet become my source in landing.
There is no cheating here.

We walk sidewalks and open doors to an air
where nothing sways
        not in the pageantry of the model's coattail
drenched in oil

        nor in the penman's court
        of action
                and emotional repercussion.

It's What We've Been Missing

A certain brand of pub culture
where the old man's milky eyes
have gone cataract
　　　glued to the football screen

where Scots shit-talk German sausage hospitals
where wasted words from some twat
　　　deemed legend by the barman

are adorned in cursive gold
high up on the wall:
So fill to me the parting glass

where women wear hoop earrings & cut-offs
rolled neatly at the fringe
exposing their scarred knees

where: *hallucinatory drugs from all tropical regions*
is carved into a wooden plaque
which might　　　in fact
switch on as a proper lamp

where mates get emotional about their dads
over slight counters
     and thick brew.

But they've got folks here who know
the secrets of the voice
one who sings at night
     to find his dead twin in the moon

his boot to the floor
     as a granddaddy timepiece

his gritty fingernails picking
     notes from scabbed memory

I wonder how many of us
     end up in their songs.

Your Room is a Campsite

yet its darkened boundaries
do not rustle of wind
through dried leaves
like the shriveled seeds of percussion.
Neither the courage of campfire
nor the howl of night slaughter lives here.
There are concrete walls
mounted with artful blocks of colored wood.
I gave you my mouth
between your double fly
in the cobblestone courtyard
where the joyrides of summer
haunt frozen bicycles.
You lunged to straighten my vertebrae
your fingers as smart nails for woodwork.
But you refused my glowy silence
my constellation curls
as signals through me.
You prefer the murkiness
which you dig out
with your crooked English teeth.
You trace my own pearly whites
with your morning thumb

nudging me against
the frigid cream-colored wall.
I would like to disappear through it
ride this room's designated ghost
to the other side
and watch you without me
in your space
greeting other women
with my hair and politics
beside the crackle of your
rolled smoking paper.

What Comes Down a Mountain

What comes down a mountain
      to meet the houses at its feet?

Ice & storm for drowning
      the tannin weight of forest.
A cathedral of trees
      fodder for puritan settlement.

The big bad mad one
gristly & growling inaudible tongue
         trading crystals & thought shapes.

Me, new in boots & spirit
the public voice of women
      stripping bark for my bite
      blowing black birdshot into the open sky
         eraser bits across a clean page.

My dear, you kept silent in the southern hemisphere
attending to your own variety
      of mountains and their brood

while I attempt sex in a museum.
My wilderness unlocked, while my
social clock winds tight
> ticking me towards the placement of oak cabinets
> the purchase of a knife set
> Rich's poems on the dreams of surgeons
> a complete cable package.

I have seen the TV Tower rendered in all mediums
> of complacent madness

from various views in the rented apartments
> of my slow departure.

Let the Snow In

I am always relieved to find myself up off the dusty floorboards, decades on from becoming a woman under you – who always let the snow in. It was more than just a motion picture, you see. It scored the lives of those who took it in. It revived the career of a mid-century fashion model who sang corners into English. It cut fabric from Glass family patterns and sewed the pilgrim's prayer to our heartbeats. It brought me home for Christmas and it sieged all my diaries, your own a childish scrawl of staff, peppered with high and low notes. The bar on Wednesday nights would play its soundtrack while you'd try to impress me by signing with the deaf man who hovered at our table. Then you'd be off again, attempting the auteur, ameliorating our lives for the GRAND COPY, stopping time in artificial moonlight through the shopping plaza trees. The night you bed me, my gray office slacks came undone to reveal tie-dye underwear I'd made from twisting cotton in small elastics. In the act, I imagined our children with too much eyeliner who suffered from the death of their genius. Then later, my memorial service where you'd let the snow in, and maybe a few flakes for my coffin. When you left the bed, I awoke curled around a bouquet of my own hands, my fingers as blades bent. Then I went home, running stumbled to the floorboards, and packed up my things 'til there was nothing left but dust.

Fall Away from Yourself

You're not always meant for motion.

Deaden the house in feather blankets
stop stirring through the sedatives.

Let your mouth undo its pain shapes.
Find your mattress to be
       the palm of the sincerest hand

melting your systems
       of coagulated blood and squeaky muscle

leading you through the
marrows of introspection.

The body beside you is changing your relationships
the moon outside you is advising.

Sleep sound as the meadow.
Fill your pockets with wheat
       watch how the wind turns its fur.

Go to crouch in the reeds
but lie down instead.

Fall away from yourself
let your limbs detach as dandelion fluff.

In space, you are a nebula thinning out its mixture.
At night, you are the slippage of a star

Come morning, listen to the sun
praising its essential violence
taking up so much room.

But we're never allowed to look.
It gives such simple instructions.

F & Z I Still Feel You

Lately, I've been seeing my fervor as a flower.
I must, because it breaks the habit of home
in perennial outburst, like how a houseguest

you haven't seen in years brightens a room.
It sits amongst my precious ornaments
and notes how adult I've become.

It must frill and color the corners of all drab things,
send gratitude across the wire, mark occasions when
days fade from the grid.

In another time where space reshapes my contours,
I drop out of school & don my navy dress. I recite
the prayer & suck back the feverish cries against

the phony. I call my brother from a massive
rotary telephone. He sits in the next room & I vex about
our family. I lay flushed, but so still, and push my

piety through the chimney of a long white cigarette.
It fills the room like a factory city, clouding the
bright busy surface of petals.

I think about all the adult things in this space
that are lowest to the ground.
They will live long lives.

It Took Us Out

past the scrappy ends of this sprawl
to the open sand where the train's window

bore the rollicking wave beyond it.
We are closer now to the laughing fires that seal

the city's messy redemption with a hot iron stoke
to the dead wood that tells us:

'don't worry, we are renewing.'
In our strangerhood we are never stranger

than the calm at the edge.
But we try to get out there

where hardcore was born in the beach's bonfire
where it's wet in October's fold.

Pink Tissue

In a bathroom, cresting the mirror,
a reflection always frames a wounded
bathtub fellow in the background
a literary work of floppy hair
with smoke and comb.

The electricity that runs the track
– the radio tower, the popsicle circuit,
the pea-brain –

makes the sound of insects busy
with a cake bake. And brushes
come to all grooves in this place and
she touches herself on that curvaceous
patch of skin between her armpit

and breast
and thinks, *how tender*.

She'd checked this spot so many times
she could draw a diagram of its knitted
network of soft pebbles. For an instant
(though ones like it had come before)
she imagines herself gone from her life

then puts herself on the phone with an
old infatuation, looking for a diagnosis:
*Love is the worst of all kinds, don't let
anyone*
tell you otherwise.

> He laughs at her
> through his nose
> above a fastened smile
> and a little to himself —
> suspects he's to blame
> for most of this.

To Prizren

A certain kind of dust has left a trail to
Prizren. She says it's like Mexico outside
as we leave the airport hanger & sit in our
stale flight clothes, fading in the highway
sun. The driver speaks his native Albanian
& offers conversational German. I accept
it gratefully & return it gracelessly.
Loose cattle are apt at crossing overpasses.
They share their kingdom with stray dogs
& proprietors of husked corn.
At matchbook junctions, like the flimsy
streets of carnival midways, storekeepers of
boy band t-shirts & fireworks shoot
strobing stares into our car seats.
Their elders wear white bucket-shaped hats
& crouch to the curb, smoking a thick
thing through a long pipe.
I read a memoir of an icon who
traveled the world, pushing beads & gems
into the graves of famous writers.

I might take a cue & wash the headstones

here of those who fought for autonomy.

But for now, we are sunk by the divisibility

of rock over region, the negotiation

between pressure & time.

I twirl my head around, looking for a

partner to rejoice in the enormity that

carries us. But she is owning the backseat

asleep against the car glass

that separates us from them.

In a Simple Room

In a simple room on the creaky bed
I did lie with MY FIRST MATE, she so still
before I could find my way to sleep.
In the next room, three other bodies
finally at rest after two days at sea.
On the maritime border, MY SECOND MATE
did ignite the music that fed the farewell
of an OLD LOVE, now a bedtime fable
flipping pages faster than a mother's recital
to reach a clean mind come morning.

Last night I opened a letter from MY LADY: she is
trying to catch a ride with fishing guides to Alaska.
This morning I put on her lover's music.
He has not sent word in months.
Thank you ABSENT LOVER OF MY LADY
for crooning about a world

too incredible

for you   ever to be able

to love.

I am grateful for such things called KEYS

that a STORMY ONE did strike when I was a

simple adolescent, when there's so much

time to be alone.

To the Much Older You

I ask,

will we ever lean against
stone statues in our perpetual garden
hot on wine after the neighbors have gone home

letting slip the jewelry we've exchanged
into the cool blue grass
and the straps off my wifely shoulder?

And if not in this lifetime

        after we've descended speedily
                down freeways
    huffing summer evening into our nostrils
        coasting on the asphalt cracked
            by ancient roots

we take to as water

      slotting coins into the viewfinder
   watching from the thorax how a bridge
           lets slip its wings

scoping as the continents split

fall and

leave us

then maybe in another

as barnyard cats
noodled together for days on end
in each other's mounds of musty fur.

After the Opera

I'm all currency   no comfort
no wild pedaling
into the city wood where Malice
would take me after the opera

spilling tales of teatimes & silk nights
with Kurdish freedom fighters.

I'd let her blanket me in myth   glide me to
velvet drawing rooms where she'd play
Russian debutante   loose bohemian
with sturdy brown heels and a bottomless
glass of sekt.

She put me to bed   then stayed for weeks
flipping crepes in the pan
        the skin of a woman
cooking turkey dinner in the nude
on Christmas Eve

before she left me in front of the movies
to get strangled in a corner bar
by a man from the Internet.

Then later, arrived on the edge of my mattress
in the gloom of the room
        donned in my white slip
a ghost I kicked in the throat
for its stare & scare.

Malice, you enchanted all my men
for revenge on your Fathers & Uncles.

Drinking wine for a thirst reserved for water.
A jukebox of autobiography   while I watched
every one of them
put another quarter   in you.

Trading Lines

Together they write poems between sheets

trading lines   in a low bed.

Two nights before my favorite day

I pressed skins with a stranger and felt

soft hair on the neck

found oats in the morning bowl

trees that busted through the boards of back porches.

The sun settled the dispute among seasons.

Hands were long and swings out-did

a busted rocking chair in theory.

I burn here.

You are a box on my thigh. I keep you there

and wash you where you like it

unsheathe you only to the seagulls

on a beach of Lake Ontario

my white flesh their holy altar.

After dinner the spoiled child and I brought our own

iconography to the chapel and executed the folk

that had been waiting from behind sticky corduroy.

In the church our knees did not get close enough.
Smoke broke the exchange of numbers in the rain
our thunder took care of the night
and dropped the heat from our skins.

I try not to relish in the flip of day for dusk
with the one who field dressed the game of
my weakened techno core.

I open to a fresh page now:

Crater	just desert
Space rock	Arbeiter
Entrance	wrought iron
Columbia	she left
Invoice	he stayed
Software	for sometimes
Trees	at first
Train	can't help it.

Your Letter Arrived

from the mouth of the post horn
as a token of your artifice.

It sailed up the rank staircase of my building
and under the timed fluorescent lights
    that go out
as a candle cries its last wax tears.

Summer had faded by the time it landed
at the end of my lace-cuffed wrists.
And from the envelope fell five fingers
    all bruised with ink.

You called each digit by name:
myself, sex, guilt, death, jokes.

I held this dismembered hand while it
took me apart
    like the wind tears clouds.
A giraffe shape becomes a broken table
    and drowns in the lake of the sky.

In MYSELF you wear a chainsaw
    for art's sake.
In SEX you watch women from the mirror
    undress in the morning light.

You're GUILTY of bathing in the smoke
    of bourbon
and in DEATH you toast the theater.

But outside the envelope, I re-assemble
the broken table
    and dress it in geraniums.
Slicing the red belly of the melon
I add a smattering of droplets
    to your seersucker
and light a fresh candle.

Over its tiny sun
we begin a whispered communion
and I am in love with this
    grand sweeping JOKE
that fell from your curated lips
    onto paper
and turned to melody
in the crescent
    of the brass horn.

They Were as Kin

They were as kin, spelling each other's names
in diner sugar, after an eternal night by the camp.

They took shelter from the southern heat in a bonfire
because it burned with the trees of cold forests

and they found the subject in the falling embers
before changing the channel with a dried branch.

At dawn, when the slimy sun took its revenge,
they would glimpse each other's halos

glinting in reflection
a brass hoop protecting a bulb

as in the altarpieces of Westphalia
where the Virgin clutches Christ to her breast

shaded only slightly by a bush
of generous roses.

The Double You

I rise to the double you
on the inside of the mattress
against the bruised wall, under the
reproductive systems of our bedspread
against the grain of bitter suitors.

All curls & coaxes, limber limbs
that scoop & squeeze.

Today I will try to be both women:
pacifist but powerful
volatile but unvarying.

You have so bravely taken me on:
a rich rewarding job, a put-out date
an enormous show of smashing atoms
embarrassed by its enormity
blind as a bat in the particle lose
a ridiculously silly affair
as we try to determine
my proper spoonfuls
the balance of my volumes:
      to pill or not to spill.

Tomorrow I rise to both of you:
stinging & sarcastic
sensuous & sincere, and O so
full of face & whiskers.

Just meters in front of us
the window bears my history
riding the lengths of greenbelts
through all this monumental stone
like Burt Lancaster in that film we saw
swimming from pool to pool
in the backyards of his wealthy neighbors
            houseless & denying his houselessness.

But you accept it warmly
like the chipped plate of nourishment
I lay before you each day.

Today is ours
under the day ghost of a satellite.
You as my tender tooth
ripping through all my proclivities.

You, waking from the outside of the bed
shrugging off your shirt

made wet from my eyes
sharing the images
your mind made last night

just beyond your delicately
shut lids.

Warmest thanks to Matthew and all the "Dead Kids" and loved ones near and far and all the places that took me out of myself and brought me home again.

Acknowledgments

Grateful acknowledgments to the following publications, in which versions of these poems appeared:

"Before I Swallowed It" was published by *Rise Up Review* in 2020.

"Radiating the Strata" was published by the *The Summerset Review* in 2020.

"What Comes Down a Mountain" was published by *Poetry Quarterly* in 2018.

"Empty Cup" was published by *Black Heart Magazine* in 2015.

"Under the Curtains" was published by *Black Heart Magazine* in 2015.

"Love is the wind stirring the grass beneath trees on a dark night" in "So Quietly" comes from Sherwood Anderson's story "Death" in *Winesburg, Ohio*.

"Blood of concentration" in "Moving Day" is borrowed from Patti Smith's book *M Train*.

"It was there I was being born" in "Innocent Railway Tunnel" is similar to "For it was there I was being borne" in Frank O'Hara's poem "River" from *Meditations in an Emergency*.

The question and response: "Is she lonely? Lonely as…" in "The Connector II" is similarly posed in Adrienne Rich's poem "Song" from *Diving into the Wreck*.

About the Author

Melanie Sevcenko is a poet, radio producer, and recovering bohemian. She moved to Portland, Oregon by way of Berlin, Germany, where she lived for almost a decade and hustled as a film critic and reporter for various outlets. Her poems have appeared in *Permafrost Magazine, Poetry Quarterly, Verse Daily, Black Heart Magazine, apt, The Fourth River,* and more. She is quite proud of the title of her poetry chapbook, *We Slept in Body Bags, Just in Case,* which was published in 2013 by Finishing Line Press. She's also an Irish and Canadian citizen and is probably a distant relative of Ukrainian writer Taras Shevchenko. These days, Melanie works in public radio and podcasting and contributes to NPR, The Guardian, and Marketplace, amongst others. In her off-time, she can be found cooking plant-based meals, lighting bonfires in backyards, or buried under her 16-pound orange tabby.

About Unsolicited Press

Unsolicited Press based out of Portland, Oregon and focuses on the works of the unsung and underrepresented. As a womxn-owned, all-volunteer small publisher that doesn't worry about profits as much as championing exceptional literature, we have the privilege of partnering with authors skirting the fringes of the lit world. We've worked with emerging and award-winning authors such as Shann Ray, Amy Shimshon-Santo, Brook Bhagat, Kris Amos, and John W. Bateman.

Learn more at unsolicitedpress.com. Find us on twitter and instagram.